Dedicated to Liberty, Divided by Power: American History to the Civil War WORKBOOK

By

ONZIÈME EDITION

Onzième Edition
PUBLISHING COMPANY

Onzième Edition
PUBLISHING COMPANY

Copyright © 2016 by Onzième Edition
US $34.95

Published by Onzième Edition.
http://www.onzieme11edition.com

ISBN 978-0-9984690-5-8

Onzième Edition is a registered trademark of Onzième Edition Publishing Company.

Inquiries go through the website: http://www.onzieme11edition.com

Printing number: 9 8 7 6 5 4 3 2 1

Printed in the United States of America

TABLE OF CONTENTS

Jennifer Morgan's essay, understandably, only contains portions of quotes form the travel narratives she employs. Examine the following quote from Richard Ligon's *True and Exact History of the Island of Barbados,* and discuss whether or not seeing the full quote changes the meaning of the quote used by Morgan. Compare & contrast Morgan's interpretation of this encounter with Ligon's full description of the encounter below in the Venn Diagram. The intersecting circles should contain what they have in common.

"FOR NOW THE PADRE AND HIS BLACK MISTRESS WERE TO TAKE TURNS. . . ON HER BODY NEXT HER LINEN, A PETTICOAT OF ORANGE TAWNY & SKY COLOR; NOT DONE WITH STRAIGHT STRIPES, BUT WAVED; AND UPON THAT A MANTLE OF PURPLE SILK, INGRAYLED WITH STRAW COLOR. THIS MANTLE WAS LARGE, AND TIED WITH A KNOT OF VERY BROAD BLACK RIBBON, WITH A RICH JEWEL ON HER RIGHT SHOULDER, WHICH CAME UNDER HER LEFT ARM . . . SHE WORE BUSKINS OF WETCHED SILK, DECKED WITH SILVER LACE, AND FRINGE; HER SHOES, OF WHITE LEATHER, LACED WITH SKY COLOR, AND PINKED BETWEEN THOSE LACES."

--RICHARD LIGON, TRUE & EXACT HISTORY, 1657

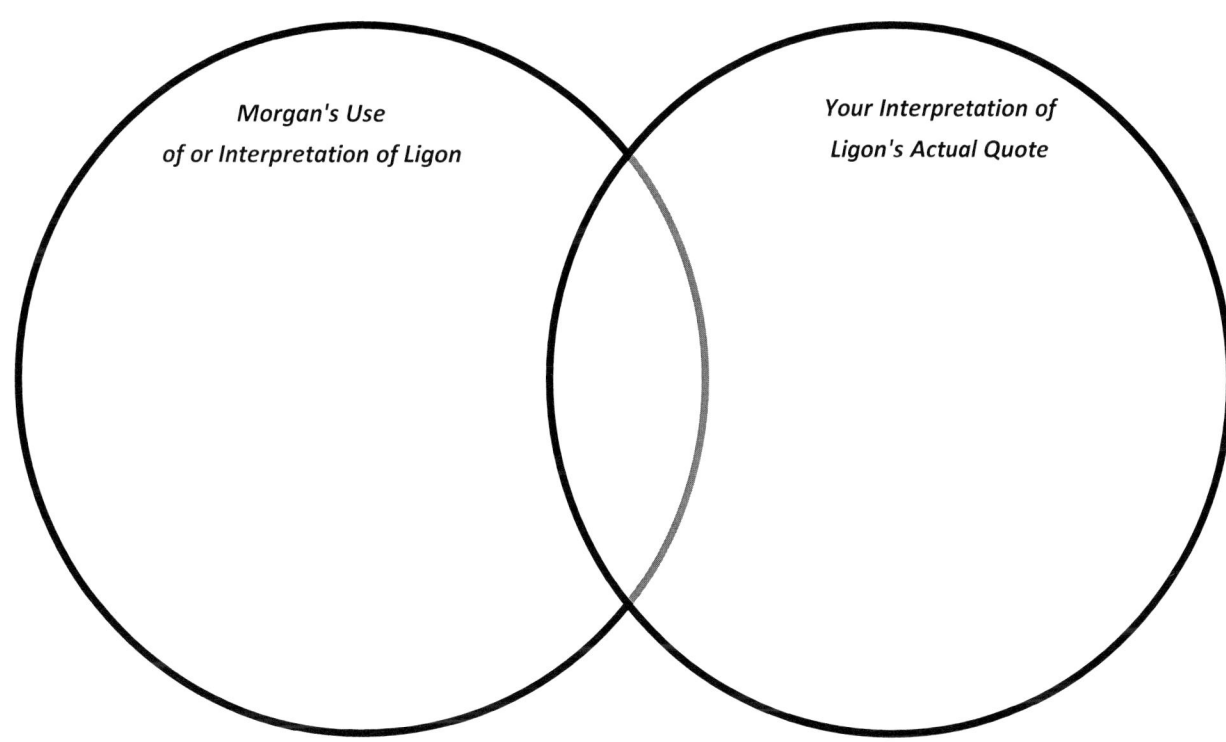

Morgan's Use of or Interpretation of Ligon

Your Interpretation of Ligon's Actual Quote

<u>Writing Assignment</u>

Due Date: _____

Requirements & Format:

- Length: 1 ½ to 3 pages
- Title for Essay (Revelatory of thesis)
- Include proper heading information: name, date, class, time, etc.
- Times New Roman Font, Size 12
- 1 inch margins
- Use in-text Citations
- MLA, APA, or Chicago Manual Style
- Works Cited
- Globalyceum may alter your format.

Objectives

- Introduce you to the examination to historiography (historians' arguments about history)
- Introduce you to the questions historians ask of sources and their authors
- Introduce you to the process of writing your own impression of the causes of American racism and slavery
- Require you to paraphrase a complex, original argument in your own words
- Encourage analysis of the various racial, ethnic and social sub-groups that played a role in the shaping of human history
- Introduce you to the historical examination and analysis of primary sources
- Introduce you to the process of writing your own account of a historical event
- Enable me to assess your writing, analytical, and organizational skills early in the semester.

Directions:

<u>Step One</u>: Read the Following Item:

Morgan, Jennifer. "'Some Could Suckle over Their Shoulder": Male Travelers, Female Bodies, and the Gendering of Racial Ideology, 1500-1770." In *William and Mary Quarterly*, Third Series, Vol. 54, No.1 (Jan., 1997), 167-192. Handed out in class. Also available on my website under History 17 articles, accessible from Class Information.

<u>Step Two (pre-writing/understanding/gathering evidence)</u>:

After reading Morgan's article, summarize both Morgan's thesis/major argument and her account of the encounter between Europeans and the indigenous/native peoples of Africa and the Americas. Be sure to include evidence from her article and the sources she uses, citing them appropriately. Be sure to include the vantage point/perspective of each group/individual involved. Be sure to discuss the sources she uses. This text is foundational to understanding the course. The assignment is intended to ensure that you grasp the contours of her argument.

Step Three:

This is just a thinking or brainstorming step. Consider these questions: How did the Europeans in Morgan's article initially perceive Africans and Native Americans? How and why did this perception change over time? How does Morgan believe Europeans justified enslaving Africans? Why, according to Morgan, did Europeans choose to enslave Africans? Again, according to Morgan, what is the relationship between gender, racism, and slavery? Are you convinced by her argument? Why or why not? Do her sources support her claims? Why? Why not? You may choose to answer your own questions or come at the sources in your own way as well. Be sure to discuss the sources she uses. Please note Morgan does not see African women as they are described in the article; she is discussing European men's supposed perception of these women in the 1500s, more than 500 years ago.

Step Four:

Complete the primary source analysis following this handout. This is required. You will turn this item in class on the day you're required to submit your essay via Globalyceum.com.

Step Five:

In a formal essay, succinctly tell the story of the origins/causes of American racism and slavery as Jennifer Morgan sees them. **Make an argument about whether or not you agree with her.** Tell me why you do or do not agree with her. Discuss the interaction between these three groups: Europeans; Africans; and Native Americans. Your summary of her argument and your thesis about whether or not you are convinced by her argument or agree with it should be in the first paragraph and be underlined. Think about writing from this perspective: to what extent can it be argued that the origins of racism and slavery in Early America resulted from the sexism and writings of a small number of European male adventurers? Summarize Jennifer Morgan's thesis, devoting your essay to arguing whether or not you agree with her and why.

Empower Yourself:

Remember to work with a free Supplemental Instructor or BC tutor and provide confirmation of it and raise your paper grade by up to 5% extra credit! Whether you fail or succeed is directly related to how hard you're willing to work and how much help you are willing to seek!

The Student Success Lab offers free writing tutorials, as well as free proofreading assistance (for papers up to 5 pages in length). The lab is open M-TH 8:30am-6:30pm and Friday 8:30-11:30am. It is located in SS 143. The tutors are exceptional! It will improve your writing. Call for an appointment: 395-4654.

The Writing Center offers free help with all steps of the writing process, except proofreading. Professional writers help with anything from understanding an assignment, to thinking out your essay, to writing it. The Center is located in Student Services 133 and can be contacted at 661-395-4735 or by email to writingcenter@bakersfieldcollege.edu

<u>Handout</u>: How to Plan, Organize, & Write an Argumentative Essay

<u>Objectives</u>: to provide a simple example of how to organize an argumentative essay, how to construct an argument, and how to support an argument

<u>Method</u>: use a simple, understandable sample to which students can refer back by memory as they structure and argue a position

<u>Background</u>: human beings are natural arguers, but many of us forget our strength in this area when we try to write arguments

<u>Part One</u>: Review the Steps to a Strong Argumentative Essay

<u>Step One</u>: Preparation work prior to writing an actual argumentative essay entails reviewing your notes, texts, etc., and brainstorming prior to the steps outlined below.

<u>Step Two</u>: Choose examples/evidence (usually key terms from texts or lecture, as well from the primary sources) that shaped the way you think about the topic.

<u>Step Three</u>: Analyze the examples/evidence, so you develop individual arguments/opinions about each example/piece of evidence. (This is where your primary source analysis form comes in handy.)

<u>Step Four</u>: Develop sub-claims, smaller arguments that, when supported, will strengthen your main argument.

<u>Step Five</u>: Make a list of the reasons each example leads you to think of and believe your sub-claim.

<u>Step Six</u>: Determine your broader conclusion from each of the arguments you developed from your evidence.

<u>Step Seven</u>: Create a thesis based on your broader conclusion.

<u>Step Eight</u>: Create an outline.

<u>Step Nine</u>: Rewrite your thesis.

<u>Step Ten</u>: Write your intro, body paragraphs, and conclusion.

<u>Step Eleven</u>: Return to your introduction; rewrite your thesis and then your entire intro.

<u>Step Twelve</u>: Rewrite the first sentence of each paragraph, making sure it's an argument.

<u>Step Thirteen</u>: Make sure each body paragraph has a sub-claim, examples and evidence, and explanations of how these examples lead you to the argument you have in the paragraph. Each paragraph should be a "mini-essay" with its own thesis (sub-claim), evidence, and explanation (analysis). As you support each sub-claim, you increase the strength of your overall thesis.

Step Fourteen: Rewrite your conclusion.

Step Fifteen: Create a title that is clever and suggests the gist of your thesis.

Step Sixteen: Read your paper out loud and make any necessary changes.

Part Two: Provide an Example of How to Do This

Example: The class wants me to bring a meal or snack to each class

Students' Initial Thesis: Bring us snacks

Their Initial sub-claims: We're hungry, we didn't have time to eat, we don't have money, etc.

Consider Your Audience & Recreate Thesis: What do they care about? What will convince them?

New Thesis: Providing a healthy snack during each class will increase student success and retention by increasing attendance, participation, focus, and retention of material.

Create an Outline:

I. Introduction
   A. Thesis: *Providing a healthy snack during each class will increase student success and retention by improving attendance, participation, focus, and retention of material.*
   B. Provide an interesting opening.
   C. Provide a "roadmap" to what you plant to discuss/how you'll lay out your essay and argument.

II. Sub-claim 1: *Students' attendance increases when snacks are available, enabling them to improve their outcome in the course.*
   A. Example/Evidence: A study of fifty community college showed that when students are forced to choose between earning money to provide for their basic needs (including food), they will choose work over school. In order to counteract this, twenty-five of the fifty test schools began making healthy snacks available at the commencement of each class. They found that attendance increased by nearly forty percent. The number of students in these colleges who succeeded in their classes improved by fifteen percent.
   B. Explain/Analysis: This study suggests that, contrary to what some instructors may think, students miss class, not because they don't care about their own education, but because they are struggling to meet their basic food and shelter needs. Once students' nutritional needs were met, they prioritized school and attended class. By attending class, they increased their exposure to course material, as well as to other students with similar goals. The number of students succeeding jumped from sixty percent to seventy-five percent.

III. Sub-claim 2: *Professors who provide snacks/meals for their students have a more collegial relationship with their students, increasing participation and collaboration.*
   A. Example/Evidence: A study out of the University of Notre Dame supports the premise that professors, who either eat with their students or bring snacks for their students, create a

more interactive class dynamic. Students shifted from the perspective that faculty experts should "share" their knowledge and students should "memorize" it to the perspective that faculty members are experts in their field that students should engage and debate with, so that students can better understand material.

    B. Explain/Analysis: Because students see their professors' commitment to them, students begin to trust, take risks in discussion, and to form bonds with those with whom they do group work. Research shows that retention increases up to ninety percent when students have the opportunity to talk about material and to teach it to others. Providing snacks creates a collegial, conversational dynamic, leading students to participate more with each other and the faculty.

IV.   Sub-Claim 3: *Students with a strong rapport with faculty are more likely to focus on lecture material, participate in group work, and strive to do well.*

    A. Example/Evidence: A leading expert in education argues that "students must know that you care before they care what you know." Her research suggests that many modern students have the impression that educators do not care about their students or their own craft, so students tend to hold faculty members in low regard and see school as something perfunctory, believing professors will just pass students along whether or not they do the assignments.

    B. Explain/Analysis: The evidence she compiles reveals that instructors who make the effort to ensure their students' needs are being met, as well as take the time to have conversations with them as they eat before class begins, earn students' respect. Because they respect their professor, students listen, participate, and engage with each other. Moreover, eating a nutritional snack prior to class stabilizes blood sugar, so students are physically able to both focus and retain information.

V.   Sub-Claim 4: *Ensuring students' nutritional needs are met increases their retention of information.*

    A. Example/Evidence: Stanford University's recent biological study on the relationship between nutrition, memory, and applying knowledge argues that in order to ensure long-term acquisition of knowledge, as well as the ability to think critically about what one learns and then apply that knowledge, is directly related to the body's nutritional levels at the time of exposure to the knowledge. Students whose nutritional needs were not met could not focus on what they were learning, could not process and understand it, and could not remember long-term or apply what they learned. Contrary to this, students who absorbed nutritionally satisfying snacks within a few minutes prior to the beginning of class overcame all of these obstacles, resulting in the ability to both critically think about what was being learned and to apply it to their world beyond the class and the particular subject.

    B. Explain/Analysis: Most professors maintain that they are experts in their field, but, in addition to teaching the subject material, they're teaching critical thinking and the application of learned knowledge. The scholarship out of Stanford University suggests that simply providing a nutritional snack to students vastly improves their chances to benefit in the short- and long-term from what they're learning.

VI.   Conclusion: (Students should reiterate/restate your thesis in a way that makes a specific appeal to your audience.)

    A.   You're a professor who values your students as human beings, and you're committed to our academic and personal success. The research examined above, as well as additional studies, overwhelmingly support the argument that instructors who provided nutritious snacks to students saw an increase in attendance and improved student interaction with material. This also facilitates student engagement in class because students realize that the instructor is invested in their well-being, encouraging them to participate more and to reach out for help when they need it. Moreover, providing nutritional snacks provides a spike in energy, and, more importantly, increased, long-term absorption of material. Providing a healthy snack to students increases the likelihood that you'll achieve the teaching goals you have for this class.

Writing Assignment Submission Checklist

1. _____ Formal essay

2. _____ Works Cited/Bibliography citing both Morgan's article and the primary sources you use from within her essay, cited as a document within an Anthology

3. _____ Properly formatted. (MLA, APA, or Chicago Manual Style)

4. _____ Creative title, suggesting your thesis

5. _____ If you work with a tutor or the writing center, type this near your title in Globalyceum

Below is a template.

(A Catchy Title that Engages and Reveals Your Thesis. Keep It Short)

I. Introduction (A, B, and C for I can be in any order.)

    A. Thesis

    _____

    _____

    _____

    _____

    B. General Context

    _____

    _____

    _____

    _____

    C. Road Map

    _____

    _____

    _____

    _____

II. First Body Paragraph

    A. 1st sentence Sub-claim

    _____

    _____

_____

_____

_____

B. Introduce Your Source

_____

_____

_____

C. Quote & Cite/Paraphrase Your Evidence

_____

_____

_____

_____

_____

D. Summarize, Interpret, and Explain

_____

_____

_____

_____

_____

III. Second Body Paragraph (Same process as II, but with different boxes)

A. 1st sentence Sub-claim:

_____

_____

_____

B. Introduce Your Source

_____

_____

_____

_____

_____

_____

C. Quote & Cite/Paraphrase Your Evidence

_____

_____

_____

_____

_____

D. Summarize, Interpret, and Explain

_____

_____

_____

_____

_____

_____

_____

IV. Third body Paragraph (Same process as II, but with different boxes)

    A. 1st sentence Sub-claim

_____

_____

_____

_____

_____

    B. Introduce Your Source

_____

_____

_____

_____

_____

    C. Quote & Cite/Paraphrase Your Evidence

_____

_____

_____

_____

_____

    D. Summarize, Interpret, and Explain

_____

_____

_____

_____

_____

_____

_____

_____

_____

_____

V. Fourth Body Paragraph (Same process as II, but with different boxes)

    A. 1st sentence Sub-claim

_____

_____

_____

_____

_____

_____

    B. Introduce Your Source

_____

_____

_____

_____

_____

    C. Quote & Cite/Paraphrase Your Evidence

_____

_____

_____

_____

_____

_____

D. Summarize, Interpret, and Explain

_____

_____

_____

_____

_____

_____

VI. Conclusion

A. Convey the significance/implications of your argument:

_____

_____

_____

_____

_____

B. Suggest further curiosities or possible future explorations:

_____

_____

_____

_____

_____

<u>Worksheet 19</u>: Roots of American Liberties   Name: _____

The Magna Carta

OBJECTIVES

Knowledge Objective: to understand the principles of liberty at the center of British, and later American, rights, as well as to understand that sometimes one group's liberties can come at the expense of another's	Skills Objective: to practice SQ4R (Survey, Question, Read, Record, Review, & Recite) in order to increase understanding of material, as well as long-term acquisition of knowledge

Thesis Question: What are the historic roots of the ideas of freedom brought to the "New World" by British explorers and settlers?

<u>Source 1:</u> The Magna Carta (1215)

Background Info: https://www.archives.gov/exhibits/featured-documents/magna-carta

Website: http://avalon.law.yale.edu/medieval/magframe.asp

Excerpt of *Magna Carta*

FIRST, THAT WE HAVE GRANTED TO GOD, and by this present charter have confirmed for us and our heirs in perpetuity, that the English Church shall be free, and shall have its rights undiminished, and its liberties unimpaired. That we wish this so to be observed, appears from the fact that of our own free will, before the outbreak of the present dispute between us and our barons, we granted and confirmed by charter the freedom of the Church's elections - a right reckoned to be of the greatest necessity and importance to it - and caused this to be confirmed by Pope Innocent III. This freedom we shall observe ourselves, and desire to be observed in good faith by our heirs in perpetuity. "

Magna Carta, 1215.

DIRECTIONS: Do a little research via the web on the *Magna Carta* and read the full document to answer the background questions. Answer in your own words.

1. **WHEN:** When was the Magna Carta written?

   _____

2. **WHERE:** Where was the Magna Carta written? _____

3. **WHAT:** What events lead to the creation of the Magna Carta?

   _____

   _____

   _____

   _____

4. **WHO:** Who played a role in the events and/or creation of the Magna Carta?

   Barons' Roles:

   _____

   _____

   _____

   King John's Role:

   _____

   _____

   _____

   _____

   Pope Innocent III's Role:

   _____

   _____

   _____

   _____

5. **WHY:** Why was this document created? (It might be helpful to think of the economic, political, religious, and military reasons central to the conflict leading to the *Magna Carta*, as well as to the resolution.)

_____

_____

_____

_____

6. **WHAT**: What are several of the rights outlined in this document? List and explain each right from the excerpts. Google and read the entire document, not just the excerpted rights.

_____

_____

_____

_____

7. **WHY:** Why do you suppose they focus so much on these specific rights?

_____

_____

_____

_____

8. **WHY:** Why does The *Magna Carta* focus significantly on property, fines, and debt? The barons seem particularly focused on the threat fines and debt impose on liberty. Do you see a relationship between fines, debt, and liberties? Explain:

_____

_____

_____

_____

9. **OPINION:** How do you think this document relates to our ideas of freedom in the modern United States?

_____

_____

_____

Objective: to understand the religious and political foundation of elected government that informed Puritan New England's society, becoming a foundation for British North America

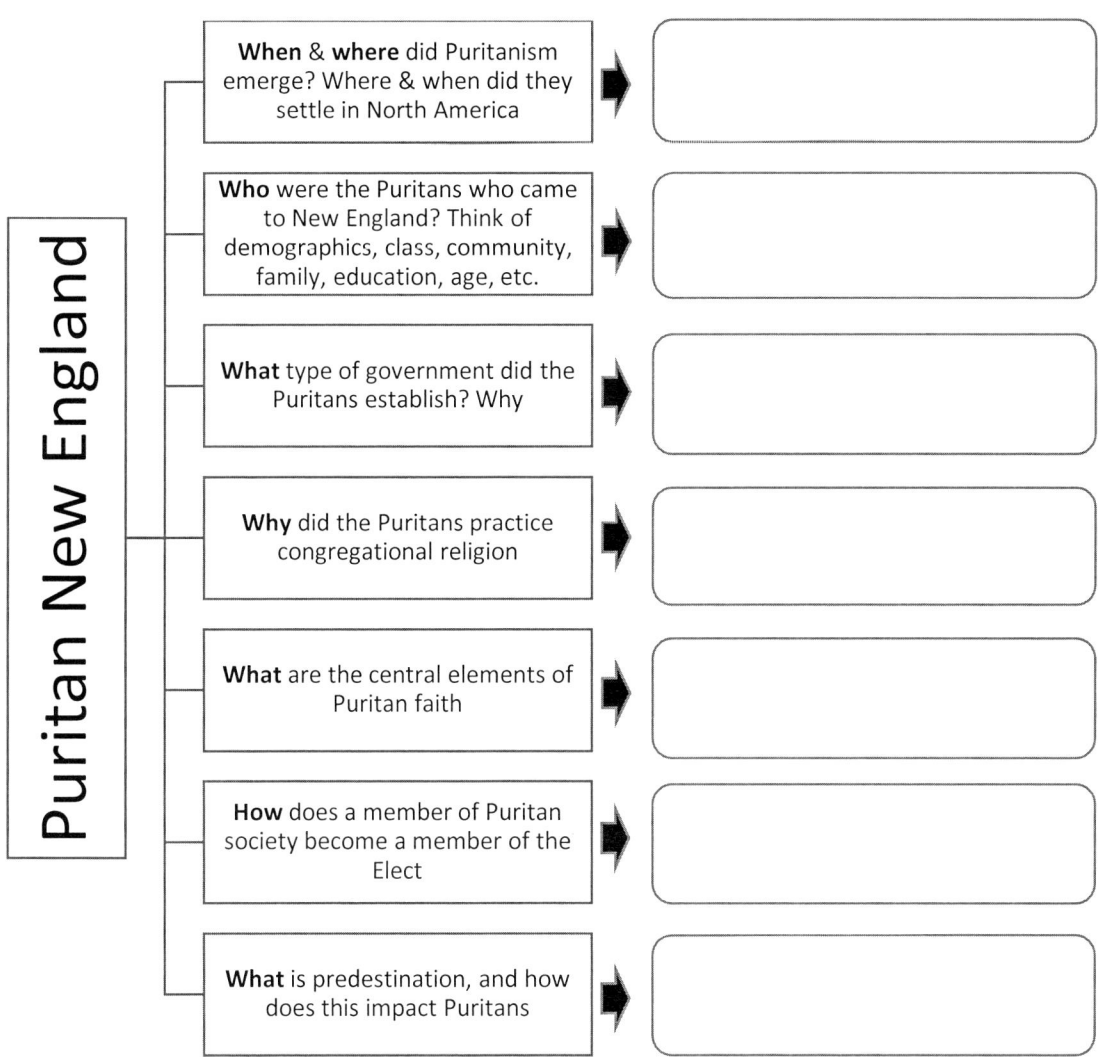

While Puritans in New England established a theocracy, how did this theocracy reflect a more democratic society and government than the one in England?

_____

_____

_____

<u>Midterm Exam Study Guide</u>   Due Date: _____

This exam has two parts, matching/fill-in-the-blank and an analysis/essay answer.

- Part I, <u>matching, has 50 questions worth one point each, totaling 50 points</u>. You will take this online via Globalyceum. You will have the week leading up to the exam to take this at home. You have two attempts; the highest score is recorded. It is timed, so work efficiently in a focused environment.
    - o There are two sections within Part I.
        - Section A is multiple choice from the Globalyceum readings/lectures key terms.
        - Section B is multiple choice from the lecture key terms.
        - You will complete Part I in class on the day of the exam.
- Part II is a primary source analysis and essay answer that draws on your knowledge from lecture and reading materials, as well as from specific primary sources.
    - o Part II is worth a combined total of 100 points.
        - <u>The analysis form, which you'll complete in advance at home is worth 25 points.</u>
        - ➢ These analyses may be completed in groups as long you name all group members on each separately submitted form and each person contributes substantially.
        - <u>The essay, which you will write in class on the day of your exam, is worth 75 points</u>. Be sure to bring one or two blank blue books from the BC bookstore. Do not write on these at all until I tell you to.
        - You will have two or three possible essay/analysis questions for which you must study.
        - There will be two to three primary sources that accompany each of the possible questions.
        - I will select two essays on the day of the exam from which you will choose to write your essay.
        - To study, reread your lecture notes and any relating texts.
        - To study, analyze the primary sources, filling out the analysis form as you go.
            - ➢ You'll work on these leading up to the exam and will be able to use them as a study guide prior to the exam. You will complete a more thorough version as part of your exam at home and turn it in at the beginning of class on exam day.
            - ➢ I suggest you complete an outline similar to the one you did on enclosure laws, but it is not required.
                - ✓ Remember, an outline should contain a thesis, sub claims, evidence/examples, and analysis/explanation. See me. I am always happy to help.
        - Arrive on time.
        - You may find many of my lecture notes and PowerPoint slides on my website, emillerbakersfieldcollege.weebly.com under Class Information, History 17A, Lecture Notes or PowerPoints.
            - ➢ My website password is Freed0m with a capital "F" and zero in place of an "o."
            - ➢ I want to remind you that I trust you to answer these questions in your own words. Don't simply copy words from the textbooks or from my notes. Imagine you're explaining the item or essay question to someone who asked you to teach them.

Part I, Section A: Study list of possible key terms from the Globalyceum essays and lectures

1. Aztecs
2. Early Atlantic Slave Trade
3. The Silk Road
4. Prince Henry, "the Navigator"
5. Slaves arrive in North America, 1518
6. *Requerimento*
7. Christopher Columbus
8. Francisco Pizarro and the Incas
9. Creole Cultures
10. Huguenots
11. English joint-stock companies
12. Newfoundland
13. Sir Walter Raleigh
14. European religious persecution and dissent
15. Peopling the Americas
16. American settlement types
17. Amerigo Vespucci
18. Latitude and Longitude
19. Ptolemy's Map
20. Pierfrancesco Lorenzo de Medici
21. Native population reduction before 1607
22. Change in Native power due to European trade
23. Separatists
24. Slavery in Barbados
25. Juan de Onate
26. Columbian Exchange
27. Black Plague/Death
28. Ricahrd Hakluyt
29. Masterless men
30. Hernan Cortes
31. Tenochtitlan
32. Roanoke Island
33. Marco Polo Travels
34. New Netherland
35. *Edmund Morgan*
36. *Jennifer Morgan*
37. Middle Ground
38. Massachusetts Bay Company
39. Puritans
40. Pilgrims
41. Roger Williams
42. King Philip's or Metacom's War
43. Iroquois Confederacy
44. Number of slaves in Virginia and Maryland compared to other colonies
45. Number of slaves imported to American colonies
46. Fur trade
47. Relationship between land and labor in Europe and America
48. Rice, sugar, and tobacco cultivation
49. Triangle trade
50. Colonial charters
51. Setters' and Natives' ideas about land ownership
52. Differences in representative assemblies in each colony
53. Differences in local government and courts in each colony
54. Differences in church and state in each colony
55. Navigation Acts
56. Survival Rates in Jamestown

Part I, Section B: Study list of possible key terms from in-class lectures

1. John Calvin
2. Henry VIII
3. Queen Mary
4. Queen Elizabeth
5. Catherine of Aragon
6. Peasants
7. Polytheistic
8. Priesthood
9. Roman Catholic Church
10. Good vs. Evil
11. *Reconquesta*
12. Church of England
23. Heads Right System
24. Iroquois Women
25. Landless Poor
26. Merchant Class
27. Martin Luther
28. Patrilineal
29. Cash Crops
30. Tobacco
31. Patriarchy
32. Granada, 1492
33. Bacon's Laws
34. Anthony Johnson
44. Isabel and Ferdinand
45. Nathaniel Bacon
46. William Berkeley
47. Crusades
48. Mercantilism
49. Laws Regulated Slaves & "Negroes"
50. Protestant Reformation
51. Gender Roles
52. Primogeniture
53. Bering Strait
54. Matrilineal

_____

_____

If you were to turn the above numbers 2 and 3, as well as the chart info into an outline, it would work something like this. (This part of the assignment is optional. You may complete the outline portion for extra credit, but I do not require you to do so.)

Below is only a model/suggestion. If it confuses you, don't use it.

(A Catchy Title that Engages and Reveals Your Thesis; Keep It Short)

I. Introduction (A, B, and C for I can be in any order.)

    A. Thesis statement from number 3 on the previous page

    B. Context of the general topic

    C. A road map to what you're going to cover/argue

II. First Body Paragraph

    A. 1st sentence should be A, B, C, or D from number 1 on the previous page. (Remember, how you choose to arrange your evidence and arguments impacts the strength of your argument. For example, think about how Jennifer Morgan used Ligon as her first and last example to prove her point that initially he saw African women as human and female, and so on.) Box 4s from chart

    B. Introduce your source from box 1 that corresponds with the box 4 you're using (A)

    C. Quote and cite your evidence, or paraphrase it if you like. This comes from box 2 that corresponds with the box 4 you use (B). Use MLA, APA, or Chicago Manuel Style of Citation; it's up to you. Be consistent.

        http://emillerbakersfieldcollege.weebly.com/help-with-citations.html

    D. Summarize, Interpret, and Explain what the evidence meant to you/how you interpret it/how your understanding lead you to argue box 1B. This is called analysis.

VII. Second body Paragraph (Same process as II, but with different boxes)

VIII. Third Body Paragraph (Same process as II, but with different boxes)

IX. Fourth Body Paragraph (Same process as II, but with different boxes)

X. Conclusion

    A. Convey the significance/implications of your argument

    B. Suggest further curiosities or possible future explorations

Below is only a model/suggestion. If it confuses you, don't use it.

(A Catchy Title that Engages and Reveals Your Thesis; Keep It Short)

I. Introduction (A, B, and C for I can be in any order.)

    A. Thesis_____

        _____

        _____

        _____

        _____

        _____

    B. General Context

        _____

        _____

        _____

        _____

        _____

        _____

    C. Road Map

        _____

        _____

        _____

        _____

        _____

        _____

        _____

II. First Body Paragraph

    A. 1st sentence Sub-claim:

        _____

        _____

        _____

        _____

B. Introduce Your Source: _____

_____

_____

_____

C. Quote & Cite/Paraphrase Your Evidence: _____

_____

_____

_____

_____

_____

D. Summarize, Interpret, and Explain: _____

_____

_____

_____

_____

_____

III. Second body Paragraph (Same process as II, but with different boxes)

A. 1st sentence Sub-claim:

_____

_____

_____

_____

_____

_____

B. Introduce Your Source:

_____

_____

_____

_____

C. Quote & Cite/Paraphrase Your Evidence: _____

_____

_____

_____

_____

_____

D. Summarize, Interpret, and Explain: _____

_____

_____

_____

_____

_____

IV. Third Body Paragraph (Same process as II, but with different boxes)

A. 1st sentence Sub-claim:

_____

_____

_____

_____

_____

_____

_____

B. Introduce Your Source: _____

_____

_____

_____

_____

_____

C. Quote & Cite/Paraphrase Your Evidence: _____

_____

_____

_____

_____

_____

_____

D. Summarize, Interpret, and Explain: _____

_____

_____

_____

_____

_____

V. Fourth Body Paragraph (Same process as II, but with different boxes)

A. 1st sentence Sub-claim:

_____

_____

_____

_____

_____

_____

_____

B. Introduce Your Source: _____

_____

_____

_____

_____

_____

C. Quote & Cite/Paraphrase Your Evidence: _____

_____

_____

_____

_____

_____

D. Summarize, Interpret, and Explain:_____

_____
_____
_____
_____
_____
_____

VI. Conclusion

    A. Convey the significance/implications of your argument:

_____
_____
_____
_____
_____

    B. Suggest further curiosities or possible future explorations:

_____
_____
_____
_____
_____

_____

_____

If you were to turn the above numbers 2 and 3, as well as the chart info into an outline, it would work something like this. (This part of the assignment is optional. You may complete the outline portion for extra credit, but I do not require you to do so.)

Below is only a model/suggestion. If it confuses you, don't use it.

(A Catchy Title that Engages and Reveals Your Thesis; Keep It Short)

I. Introduction (A, B, and C for I can be in any order.)

    A. Thesis statement from number 3 on the previous page

    B. Context of the general topic

    C. A road map to what you're going to cover/argue

II. First Body Paragraph

    A. 1st sentence should be A, B, C, or D from number 1 on the previous page. (Remember, how you choose to arrange your evidence and arguments impacts the strength of your argument. For example, think about how Jennifer Morgan used Ligon as her first and last example to prove her point that initially he saw African women as human and female, and so on.) Box 4s from chart

    B. Introduce your source from box 1 that corresponds with the box 4 you're using (A)

    C. Quote and cite your evidence, or paraphrase it if you like. This comes from box 2 that corresponds with the box 4 you use (B). Use MLA, APA, or Chicago Manuel Style of Citation; it's up to you. Be consistent.

    http://emillerbakersfieldcollege.weebly.com/help-with-citations.html

    D. Summarize, Interpret, and Explain what the evidence meant to you/how you interpret it/how your understanding lead you to argue box 1B. This is called analysis.

III. Second body Paragraph (Same process as II, but with different boxes)

IV. Third Body Paragraph (Same process as II, but with different boxes)

V. Fourth Body Paragraph (Same process as II, but with different boxes)

VI. Conclusion

    A. Convey the significance/implications of your argument

    B. Suggest further curiosities or possible future explorations

Below is only a model/suggestion. If it confuses you, don't use it.

(A Catchy Title that Engages and Reveals Your Thesis; Keep It Short)

I. Introduction (A, B, and C for I can be in any order.)

A. Thesis_____

_____

_____

_____

_____

_____

_____

B. General Context

_____

_____

_____

_____

_____

_____

C. Road Map

_____

_____

_____

_____

_____

_____

II. First Body Paragraph

A. 1st sentence Sub-claim:

_____

_____

_____

_____

B. Introduce Your Source: _____

C. Quote & Cite/Paraphrase Your Evidence: _____

_____

_____

_____

_____

_____

D. Summarize, Interpret, and Explain: _____

_____

_____

_____

_____

_____

III. Second body Paragraph (Same process as II, but with different boxes)

A. 1st sentence Sub-claim:

_____

_____

_____

_____

_____

_____

B. Introduce Your Source:

_____

_____

_____

_____

C. Quote & Cite/Paraphrase Your Evidence:

_____

_____

_____

_____

_____

_____

_____

D. Summarize, Interpret, and Explain: _____

_____

_____

_____

_____

_____

IV. Third Body Paragraph (Same process as II, but with different boxes)

A. 1ˢᵗ sentence Sub-claim:

_____

_____

_____

_____

_____

_____

B. Introduce Your Source: _____

_____

_____

_____

_____

_____

C. Quote & Cite/Paraphrase Your Evidence: _____

_____

_____

_____

_____

_____

_____

D. Summarize, Interpret, and Explain: _____

_____

_____

_____

_____

_____

V. Fourth Body Paragraph (Same process as II, but with different boxes)

A. 1st sentence Sub-claim:

_____

_____

_____

_____

_____

_____

B. Introduce Your Source: _____

_____

_____

_____

_____

_____

C. Quote & Cite/Paraphrase Your Evidence: _____

_____

_____

_____

_____

_____

D. Summarize, Interpret, and Explain:_____

_____

_____

_____

_____

_____

VI. Conclusion

    A. Convey the significance/implications of your argument:

_____

_____

_____

_____

_____

    B. Suggest further curiosities or possible future explorations:

_____

_____

_____

_____

_____

<u>Debate Handout:</u> Thomas Jefferson's Democratic Republicans vs. Alexander Hamilton's Federalists

Objectives: to understand the leadership style of George Washington, as well as the ideological scaffolding that shaped our early nation, as well as the continued debates between political parties

Assignment: Two sides will debate the positions of Thomas Jefferson and Alexander Hamilton, as well as their political parties, the Democratic Republicans and the Federalists. I've listed the primary source documents that argue both sides, as well as key events, individuals, and organizations that represent the arguments and views of both sides below. Your assignment collectively and individually is to build an argument and evidence on behalf of the side you've chosen/been assigned. Certain people must choose to take on identities, such as Thomas Jefferson, Alexander Hamilton, James Madison, and George Washington, etc. In addition to being prepared to argue the merits or faults of either side, you should anticipate the other side's refutations and be able to counter them. The debate is organized thematically, so we can adequately cover all key points. One person will act as George Washington, who will arbitrate the debate. Two individuals, one on each side, will act as Jefferson and Hamilton. Washington starts the debate by inviting Jefferson and Hamilton to advise him. Washington, Jefferson, and Hamilton, as well as James Madison will each introduce themselves, providing biography, etc. Then we will move on to debate the economic, military, western expansion, political (role of the government), and ideological policy differences between Jefferson and Hamilton, as well as debate their views on "the common man". The goal is for either side to get Washington to side with them on policy decisions.

A couple of great general links with info:

http://americanhistory.unomaha.edu/module_display.php?mod_id=127&review=yes

http://chnm.gmu.edu/exploring/19thcentury/debateoverslavery/assignment.php

*This is a historical debate argued from the perspective of the people at the time.

    I.   Introductions, Bios, and Perspectives
        A. George Washington
            1. Links to Bios on Washington:
            2. http://www.mountvernon.org/george-washington/biography/
            3. https://www.whitehouse.gov/1600/presidents/georgewashington
        B. Alexander Hamilton
            1. Links to Bios on Hamilton
            2. https://www.congress.gov/resources/display/content/The+Federalist+Papers
            3. http://www.ushistory.org/valleyforge/served/hamilton.html
            4. http://law2.umkc.edu/faculty/projects/ftrials/burr/HamiltonBio.htm
            5. http://www.pbs.org/wgbh/amex/hamilton/peopleevents/e_federalist.html
            6. http://www.pbs.org/wgbh/amex/hamilton/timeline/
            7. http://www.pbslearningmedia.org/resource/arct14.soc.amexdulham/the-duel-hamilton-and-the-us-constitution/
        C. Thomas Jefferson
            1. Links to Bios on Jefferson
            2. https://www.monticello.org/site/jefferson/thomas-jefferson-brief-biography
            3. Https://www.whitehouse.gov/1600/presidents/thomasjefferson

4. Jefferson's Role in the Washington & Adams Administrations: http://www.loc.gov/teachers/classroommaterials/connections/thomas-jefferson/history5.html
5. Jefferson's Overall Political Ideology: http://www.ushistory.org/us/20b.asp
6. Jefferson's Concern Over the Political Climate: http://www.loc.gov/item/mtjbib008657/
7. http://www.pbs.org/wgbh/amex/duel/peopleevents/pande07.html
8. http://www.pbs.org/wgbh/aia/part3/3h490t.html

D. James Madison
1. Links to Bios on Madison:
2. https://www.montpelier.org/james-and-dolley-madison/james-madison/bio
3. https://www.whitehouse.gov/1600/presidents/jamesmadison

II. Federalists Party Background
   A. http://www.history.com/topics/federalist-party
   B. http://www.ushistory.org/us/16a.asp
   C. http://www.pbs.org/wgbh/amex/duel/peopleevents/pande05.html
   D. Hamilton's Federalist Views a Summary: http://www.pbs.org/wgbh/amex/hamilton/peopleevents/e_federalist.html
   E. http://www.constitution.org/fed/federa00.htm
   F. http://teachingamericanhistory.org/fed-antifed/

III. Democratic-Republican Party Background
   A. Anti-federalists: http://www.ushistory.org/us/16b.asp
   B. Anti-federalists: http://teachingamericanhistory.org/fed-antifed/antifederalist/
   C. http://teachingamericanhistory.org/fed-antifed/the-antifederalists/
   D. http://www.u-s-history.com/pages/h446.html
   E. http://www.pbs.org/wgbh/amex/duel/peopleevents/pande09.html
   F. http://ic.galegroup.com/ic/uhic/ReferenceDetailsPage/DocumentToolsPortletWindow?displayGroupName=Reference&jsid=f09a642e26f9a5c7f1699d76ab91d29d&action=2&catId=&documentId=GALE|CX3427300057&u=oak30216&zid=e44f52f1a22c74655a30c2679aac4084
   G. Comparison: https://www.gilderlehrman.org/history-by-era/creating-new-government/resources/differences-between-federalists-and-antifederalists
   H. https://www.gilderlehrman.org/history-by-era/creating-new-government/essays/antifederalists-other-founders-american-constitutional
   I. http://ic.galegroup.com/ic/uhic/ReferenceDetailsPage/DocumentToolsPortletWindow?displayGroupName=Reference&jsid=27c4d7c605ee78f96be9be874b8f557c&action=2&catId=&documentId=GALE|CX3048900171&u=oak30216&zid=9c00b8eb644b4e46de39f8a9335adc67
   J. For the Debate Lover: Jefferson's *Notes on Virginia*:
   K. Jefferson Quotes and Family Letters: http://tjrs.monticello.org/archive/search/quotes?keys=&field_tjrs_categorization_tid[]=2179

IV. A General Comparison of Hamilton/Federalists and Jefferson/Democratic Republicans
   A. Charts Comparing Hamilton & Jefferson:
      https://www.google.com/search?q=charts+comparing+alexander+hamilton+and+thomas+jefferson&biw=1525&bih=734&source=lnms&tbm=isch&sa=X&ved=0CAYQ_AUoAWoVChMIkJzjz_L0yAIVTHY-Ch1hOgxh&dpr=0.9
   B. A Detailed Comparison of the Two Men:
      http://mrfarshtey.net/notes/HamiltonvsJefferson.pdf
   C. Jefferson vs. Hamilton Debate: reenacted: http://www.c-span.org/video/?161239-1/jeffersonhamilton-debate-reenactment
   D. Federalists Papers (http://www.let.rug.nl/usa/documents/1786-1800/the-federalist-papers/)
   E. https://sites.google.com/site/ourhistoryproject13/to-dos

V. Constitutional Interpretations & Views of the Role of the Federal Government/Political Ideology
   A. Hamilton's Loose Interpretation of the Constitution
      1. Hamilton & Limiting the Free Press: http://press-pubs.uchicago.edu/founders/documents/bill_of_rightss7.html
      2. https://www.congress.gov/resources/display/content/The+Federalist+Papers#TheFederalistPapers-21
      3. Whiskey Rebellion Background: http://www.digitalhistory.uh.edu/teachers/lesson_plans/pdfs/unit3_5.pdf
      4. http://www.pbs.org/wgbh/amex/duel/sfeature/hamiltonusconstituion.html
      5. Madison, Powers Conferred By Constitution: https://www.congress.gov/resources/display/content/The+Federalist+Papers#TheFederalistPapers-41
      6. Madison, Conformity of Plan with Republican Principles: https://www.congress.gov/resources/display/content/The+Federalist+Papers#TheFederalistPapers-39
      7. Madison, Powers Conferred by the Constitution #2: https://www.congress.gov/resources/display/content/The+Federalist+Papers#TheFederalistPapers-42

   B. Jefferson's Strict Interpretation of the Constitution
      1. Whiskey Rebellion Background: http://www.digitalhistory.uh.edu/teachers/lesson_plans/pdfs/unit3_5.pdf
      2. Jefferson's Reaction to the Whiskey Rebellion: http://lcweb2.loc.gov/service/mss/mtj//mtj1/020/020_0314_0317.pdf
      3. Jefferson on Limiting Federal Power: http://www.loc.gov/exhibits/jefferson/jefffed.html
      4. Jefferson on the 2nd Amendment: http://www.monticello.org/site/jefferson/beauty-second-amendment-quotation & https://www.thefederalistpapers.org/history/the-founding-fathers-on-the-second-amendment
      5. https://www.loc.gov/exhibits/jefferson/jefffed.html
      6. http://www.thefederalistpapers.org/anti-federalist-papers

VI.   Role of the Military
   A. Hamilton on the Military
       1. https://www.congress.gov/resources/display/content/The+Federalist+Papers#TheFederalistPapers-11
       2. https://www.congress.gov/resources/display/content/The+Federalist+Papers#TheFederalistPapers-24
       3. https://www.congress.gov/resources/display/content/The+Federalist+Papers#TheFederalistPapers-25
       4. https://www.congress.gov/resources/display/content/The+Federalist+Papers#TheFederalistPapers-26
       5. https://www.congress.gov/resources/display/content/The+Federalist+Papers#TheFederalistPapers-27
       6. https://www.congress.gov/resources/display/content/The+Federalist+Papers#TheFederalistPapers-28
       7. https://www.congress.gov/resources/display/content/The+Federalist+Papers#TheFederalistPapers-29
   B. Jefferson on the Military
       1. http://founders.archives.gov/documents/Jefferson/03-07-02-0471
       2. http://lehrmaninstitute.org/history/foundingeconomists.html#military

VII.   Economic Plans
   A. Hamilton & the Federalists
       1. Hamilton's Financial Plan: http://www.ushistory.org/us/18b.asp
       2. Summary Hamilton's Financial Plan: http://www.ushistory.org/us/18b.asp &
           http://www.digitalhistory.uh.edu/disp_textbook.cfm?smtID=2&psid=2973
       3. Background on Hamilton's Manufacturing:
           http://www.brookings.edu/research/articles/2011/12/05-manufacturing-katz-lee
       4. Hamilton on Manufacturing: https://www.gilderlehrman.org/history-by-era/early-republic/resources/hamilton%E2%80%99s-report-subject-manufactures-1791 &
           http://www.let.rug.nl/usa/biographies/alexander-hamilton/report-on-manufactures---submitted-to-congress-december-5-1791.php
       5. Hamilton on Taxes 1:
           https://www.congress.gov/resources/display/content/The+Federalist+Papers#TheFederalistPapers-30
       6. Hamilton on Taxes 2:
           https://www.congress.gov/resources/display/content/The+Federalist+Papers#TheFederalistPapers-31
       7. Hamilton on Taxes 3:
           https://www.congress.gov/resources/display/content/The+Federalist+Papers#TheFederalistPapers-32
       8. Hamilton on Taxes 4:
           https://www.congress.gov/resources/display/content/The+Federalist+Papers#TheFederalistPapers-33 (Students Responsible:
           _____)
       9. Hamilton on Taxes 5:
           https://www.congress.gov/resources/display/content/The+Federalist+Papers#TheFederalistPapers-34

10. Hamilton on Taxes 6: https://www.congress.gov/resources/display/content/The+Federalist+Papers#TheFederalistPapers-35
11. Hamilton on Taxes 7: https://www.congress.gov/resources/display/content/The+Federalist+Papers#TheFederalistPapers-36
12. Hamilton on the National Bank: http://history.hanover.edu/courses/excerpts/111hamilton.html
13. https://www.congress.gov/resources/display/content/The+Federalist+Papers#TheFederalistPapers-12
14. https://www.congress.gov/resources/display/content/The+Federalist+Papers#TheFederalistPapers-13
15. Summary of Hamilton and Jefferson on the National Bank: http://www.digitalhistory.uh.edu/teachers/lesson_plans/pdfs/unit3_4.pdf

16. Video Clips: http://www.pbs.org/wgbh/amex/hamilton/sfeature/scenes.html#bank

B. Jefferson & the Democratic Republicans
   1. Jefferson Against the National Bank: http://avalon.law.yale.edu/18th_century/bank-tj.asp
   2. Summary Jefferson & Hamilton on the National Bank: http://www.digitalhistory.uh.edu/teachers/lesson_plans/pdfs/unit3_4.pdf
   3. Jefferson on Banks: https://www.monticello.org/site/jefferson/private-banks-quotation
   4. Jefferson on Being a Farming/Agrarian Nation: http://www.historytools.org/sources/Jefferson-agrarianism.pdf
   5. Edmund Morgan's article on American Slavery, American Freedom.
   6. Video Clips: http://www.pbs.org/wgbh/amex/hamilton/sfeature/scenes.html#bank

VIII. Views of Westward Expansion
   A. Hamilton's Views:
      1. Look them up
   B. Jefferson's Views:
      1. http://www.ushistory.org/us/20c.asp
      2. https://www.loc.gov/exhibits/jefferson/jeffwest.html (Several Great Primary Sources Here)
      3. http://jeffersonswest.unl.edu/thematic/expansion.php
      4. https://www.monticello.org/site/jefferson/lewis-and-clark-expedition
   C. Northwest Ordinance: http://www.let.rug.nl/usa/documents/1786-1800/the-northwest-ordinance-july-13-1787.php
   D. General: http://lehrmaninstitute.org/history/founders-land.html#knox
   E. Excellent Source: http://lehrmaninstitute.org/history/foundingeconomists.html

IX. Views of the Common Man
   A. Jefferson's Views:
      1. A General Bill for the Diffusion of Knowledge: https://www.monticello.org/site/jefferson/bill-more-general-diffusion-knowledge
      2. Jefferson on Religion and Common Man: http://www.vahistorical.org/collections-and-resources/virginia-history-explorer/thomas-jefferson

3. On Education and Freedom:
   https://www.history.org/Media/flash/Jefferson/report.htm
4. Thomas Paine, the Rights of Man: http://www.let.rug.nl/usa/documents/1786-1800/thomas-paine-the-rights-of-man/
B. Hamilton's Views:
   1. http://lehrmaninstitute.org/history/foundingeconomists.html#democracy
   2. http://www.ourrepubliconline.com/Author/22
   3. http://www.pbs.org/wgbh/amex/hamilton/filmmore/pt_2.html
   4. http://www.pbs.org/wgbh/amex/hamilton/sfeature/scenes_02_trans.html

X.   Hamilton's and Jefferson's Relationships with Washington
A. Some Context to The Relationship Between Washington, Hamilton, and Jefferson:
   http://www.loc.gov/teachers/classroommaterials/connections/thomas-jefferson/history5.html

XI. Trials, Laws, & Executive Acts
A. Articles of Confederation: http://www.constitution.org/cons/usa-conf.htm
B. Sedition Act Trials: http://www.fjc.gov/history/home.nsf/page/tu_sedbio_fr.html
C. Marbury vs. Madison:
   http://www.pbs.org/wnet/supremecourt/democracy/landmark_marbury.html
D. Federalist Court: http://www.ushistory.org/us/20e.asp
E. Declaration of Independence: Jefferson's *Declaration of Independence*:
   http://billofrightsinstitute.org/founding-documents/declaration-of-independence/
F. Bill of Rights: http://www.billofrightsinstitute.org/founding-documents/bill-of-rights/
G. Bill of Rights 2: https://www.docsoffreedom.org/readings/the-bill-of-rights
H. Bill of Rights 3: http://www.let.rug.nl/usa/documents/1786-1800/madison-speech-proposing-the-bill-of-rights-june-8-1789.php
I. Second Amendment: https://www.thefederalistpapers.org/history/the-founding-fathers-on-the-second-amendment
J. Jefferson on the 2nd Amendment: http://www.monticello.org/site/jefferson/beauty-second-amendment-quotation & https://www.thefederalistpapers.org/history/the-founding-fathers-on-the-second-amendment
K. Ninth & Tenth Amendments of the Bill of Rights:
   1. Amendment IX: The enumeration in the Constitution, of certain rights, shall not be construed to deny or disparage others retained by the people.
   2. Amendment X: The powers not delegated to the United States by the Constitution, nor prohibited by it to the states, are reserved to the states respectively, or to the people.

XII. General Steps
A. Read a brief biography on both Alexander Hamilton and Thomas Jefferson, as well as reading summaries of Federalists and Democratic-Republicans/Jeffersonian Republicans.
B. Decide which ones political and economic views you think would be better for the people and the nation during that time
C. Look at some of the documents under the side you are most interested in. Read them. Take notes.

D. Get together with your team and divide up the documents/key terms, so that you have several "experts" for each item

E. You should read all of the documents if possible, at least skimming over them, but become an expert on a few for your side, as well as for the opposition's sides, so you can challenge them.

F. Complete the Debate Preparation Template (This is worth 50 points)

XIII.   Debate Format

A. Divide into Teams.

B. Determine that someone is an "expert" on each term.

C. Create three to five main arguments that demonstrate your team's strengths.

D. Create three to five arguments against the opposing team.

E. Use your "terms" as evidence to support your main arguments.

F. Anticipate how the other side will attack you and create a defense.

Debate Handout: Historical Pro- vs. Anti-Slavery Debate

Objectives: to understand the economic, political, pseudo-scientific, and religious arguments for and against slavery from the perspective of the people at the time

Two sides will debate the positions of antebellum Americans for and against slavery (pro- vs. anti-slavery). I've listed the primary source documents that argue both sides, as well as key events, individuals, and organizations that represent the arguments and views of both sides below. Your assignment collectively and individually is to build an argument and evidence on behalf of the side you've chosen/been assigned. Certain people must choose to take on identities, such as John C. Calhoun, David Walker, Frederick Douglass, etc. In addition to being prepared to argue the merits or faults of either side, you should anticipate the other side's refutations and be able to counter them.

A couple of great general links with info:

http://americanhistory.unomaha.edu/module_display.php?mod_id=127&review=yes

http://chnm.gmu.edu/exploring/19thcentury/debateoverslavery/assignment.php

*This is a historical debate argued from the perspective of the people at the time. We are not arguing whether or not we would have been or are for or against slavery today. We are arguing as the people did in the past over the institution of slavery.

I. Debate: Pro- vs Anti-Slavery

   A. Religious key terms/evidence for and against slavery
      1. Religious key terms/evidence against slavery
         a. William Wilson
         b. "The Great American Question" http://memory.loc.gov/cgi-bin/query/r?ammem/rbaapc:@field%28DOCID+@lit%28rbaapc34000div0%29%29
         c. Anti-Slavery Manual http://babel.hathitrust.org/cgi/pt?id=loc.ark:/13960/t5gb2679p;view=1up;seq=33
         d. Sunderland LaRoy
         e. American Anti-Slavery Society
         f. American Anti-Slavery Society Constitutionhttp://chnm.gmu.edu/exploring/19thcentury/debateoverslavery/pop_antislavery_society.html
         g. Johnathan Edwards
         h. Edwards, "Injustice and Impolicy of the Slavery Trade" https://archive.org/stream/injusticeimpolic02lcedwa/injusticeimpolic02lcedwa_djvu.txt
      2. Religious key terms/evidence in favor of slavery
         a. George Freeman
         b. The Rights and Duties of Slaveholders http://www1.assumption.edu/users/lknoles/douglassproslaveryargs.html
         c. Nellie Norton, Southern Slavery and the Biblehttp://docsouth.unc.edu/imls/warren/menu.html

  d. Thorton Stringfellow

  e. Brief Examination of Scripture Testimony on the Institution of Slavery
   http://memory.loc.gov/cgi-bin/query/r?ammem/rbaapc:@field%28DOCID+@lit%28rbaapc28100div0%29%29

  f, The Staunton Spectator
   http://chnm.gmu.edu/exploring/19thcentury/debateoverslavery/pop_spectator1.html

B. Political key terms/evidence for and against slavery

 1. Political key terms/evidence against slavery

  a. David Wilmot

  b. Wilmot Proviso http://dig.lib.niu.edu/teachers/politics-platform-d.html

  c. Liberty Party Platform

  d. Daniel Webster http://www.mtholyoke.edu/acad/intrel/wilmot.htm

  e. Webster Remarks http://memory.loc.gov/cgi-bin/query/r?ammem

  f. The Free Soil Movement

  g. Free Soil Party Platform 1848 http://dig.lib.niu.edu/teachers/politics-platform-e.html

  h. Frederick Douglass's views of Free Soilers
   http://docsouth.unc.edu/neh/dougl92/dougl92.html#p337

  i. Stephen Douglas

  j. Stephen Douglas on slavery
   http://facweb.furman.edu/~benson/docs/Douglas50.htm

  k. Constitutional End to the International Slave Trade in 1808

  l. Northwest Ordinance of 1787

 2. Political key terms/evidence in favor of slavery

  a. John C. Calhoun

  b. "Slavery as a Positive Good"
   http://www.assumption.edu/ahc/abolition/CalhounPositiveGood.html

  c. "Disquisition on Government" http://www.constitution.org/jcc/disq_gov.htm

  d. Calhoun's Southern Address
   http://facweb.furman.edu/~benson/docs/calhoun.htm

  e. George Fitzhugh

  f. Fitzhugh, Cannibals All
   http://chnm.gmu.edu/exploring/19thcentury/debateoverslavery/pop_fitzhugh.html

  g. Theodore Weld

  h. Weld, American Slavery as it is
   http://chnm.gmu.edu/exploring/19thcentury/debateoverslavery/pop_weld.html

  i. Dred Scott Decision

  j. 3/5th Compromise

C. Economic key terms/evidence for and against slavery

 1. Economic key terms/evidence against slavery

  a. Hinton Helper

  b. Helper anti-slavery argument http://docsouth.unc.edu/nc/helper/helper.html

  c. Jesse Burton Harrison

  d. Burton on anti-slavery http://archive.oah.org/special-issues/teaching/2008_06/sources/ex3_b1.html

2. Economic key terms/evidence in favor of slavery
   a. Edmund Ruffin
   b. Ruffin Pro-Slavery argument: http://memory.loc.gov/cgi-bin/query/r?ammem/rbaapc:@field%28DOCID+@lit%28rbaapc25000div0%29%29
   c. Arguments from the book *Time on the Cross*, *http://www.sjsu.edu/faculty/watkins/fogel.htm*
   d. J.D. B. De Bow
   e. De Bow the Industrial Resources: http://chnm.gmu.edu/exploring/19thcentury/debateoverslavery/pop_debow.html
   f. The Spectator, part two http://chnm.gmu.edu/exploring/19thcentury/debateoverslavery/pop_spectator2.html

D. Abolitionists, Free Soilers, Anti-Slavery Folks, and Pro-Slavery Folks
   1. Abolitionists
      a. William Lloyd Garrison
      b. Elijah Lovejoy
      c. Harriet Beecher Stowe
      d. Elizabeth Cady Stanton
      e. Susan B. Anthony
      f. John Brown
      g. Charles Sumner
      h. Thaddeus Stevens
      i. Grimke Sisters

   2. Abolitionists who were former Slaves
      a. Henry Highland Garnett
      b. Garnett's Speech http://www.pbs.org/wgbh/aia/part4/4h2937t.html
      c. Frederick Douglass
      d. Douglass's Narrative
      e. Douglass's letter to Garrison http://docsouth.unc.edu/neh/douglass/support12.html
      f. Douglass "Inhumanity of Slavery" http://docsouth.unc.edu/neh/douglass55/douglass55.html#p435
      g. Douglass, Spread Light on American Slavery: http://chnm.gmu.edu/exploring/19thcentury/debateoverslavery/pop_douglass.html
      h. Harriet Jacobs
      i. William Wells Brown
      j. Narrative of William Wells Brown http://docsouth.unc.edu/neh/brown47/brown47.html
   3. Free Soilers
      a. Abraham Lincoln
   4. Anti-Slavery
      a. Thomas Jefferson
      b. Benjamin Franklin
      c. Tom Paine

        d. John Jay
        e. American Colonization Soceity
    5. Pro Slavery
        a. James Thornwell
        b. Nellie Norton
        c. James Henry Hammond (Mudsill Speech)
        d. John C. Calhoun
        e. Thomas Dew (A Review of the Debates in the Legislature)
        f. Samuel Cartwright
        g. William Harper
        h. Harper, Memoir of Slavery
           https://archive.org/stream/memoirofslaveryr02harp/memoirofslaveryr02harp_dj
           vu.txt
    6. Militants
        a. David Walker
        b. Walker's Appeal
        c. Nat Turner
        d. Turner's Rebellion
E. Pseudo-Science Arguments
    1. Pseudo-science in favor of slavery
        a. Samuel Morton
        b. Morton, Crania Americana
           http://chnm.gmu.edu/exploring/19thcentury/debateoverslavery/pop_morton.ht
           ml
        c. James Hunt
        d. Hunt, "The Negro's Place in Nature"
           https://archive.org/details/negrosplaceinna00huntgoog

---

General Steps

1. Read a brief summary of your key terms after searching them on Google.
2. Get together with your team and divide up the documents/key terms, so that you have several "experts" for each item.
3. You should read all of the documents if possible, at least skimming over them, but become an expert on a few for your side, as well as for the opposition's sides, so you can challenge them.
4. Complete the Debate Preparation Template (This is worth 50 points)

Preparing for the Debate

1. Divide into Teams.
2. Choose a few leaders per team.
3. Determine who wants to focus on which of the following themes within the debate, religious arguments for and against slavery, economic arguments for and against slavery, pseudo-science arguments for and against slavery, and political arguments for and against slavery.
4. Appoint one leader to each of these four themes. (It might help to have an overall leader as well.)
5. Assign/choose at least three individuals to cover each key term/person etc.
6. People should be responsible for knowing at least three aspects on their side and on the opposing side.
7. Study your key terms.
8. Get into character.
9. Study your key terms.
10. Pull several quotes that are powerful to you in order to use them in the debate. During the debate be able to explain what they mean to your character.
11. Individually create three to five main arguments, using the debate prep/primary source analysis form, in favor of the key terms that represent the key terms for each individual's key terms.
12. Individually create three to five main arguments, using the debate prep/primary source analysis form, arguing against the key terms you studied for the opposing side.
13. Collectively create three to five main arguments that support your side's views.
14. Create three to five arguments against the opposing team's views, using your knowledge of their key terms to do this.
15. Use your "terms" as evidence to support your main arguments.
16. Anticipate how the other side will attack you and create a defense.

<u>Worksheet 40</u>: Debate Template for Slavery vs. Anti-Slavery Debate

Name: _____

Side of the Debate You Chose: _____

List the Examples & Evidence You Plan to USE to Support Your Side of the Debate:

1. _____

2. _____

3. _____

4. _____

Summarize Each Example & Source Here and/or Staple Your <u>Handwritten</u> Work to this Paper:

_____

_____

_____

_____

_____

_____

_____

_____

_____

_____

List the Examples & Evidence You Plan to USE to REFUTE Your Opponents:

1. _____

    _____

2. _____

    _____

3. _____

_____

4. _____

_____

Summarize Each:

_____

_____

_____

_____

_____

_____

_____

_____

_____

_____

List Three Main Arguments Stating YOUR Side's Position:

1. _____

2. _____

3. _____

List Three Main Arguments Attacking Your OPPONENT'S Position:

1. _____

2. _____

3. _____

Anticipate Three Argument's Your Opponent's Side Will Make Against YOU:

1. _____

2. _____

3. _____

Create Three Rebuttals to the Arguments You Believe Your Opponent Will Make Against You:

1. _____

2. _____

3. _____

Additional Info:

_____

_____

_____

_____

_____

_____

_____

_____

_____

_____

_____

_____

_____

_____

Worksheet 41: Slavery & Compromise   Name:_____

Objective: to understand the precarious balance of power & the comprises intended to maintain this balance from the formation of the United States to the Civil War

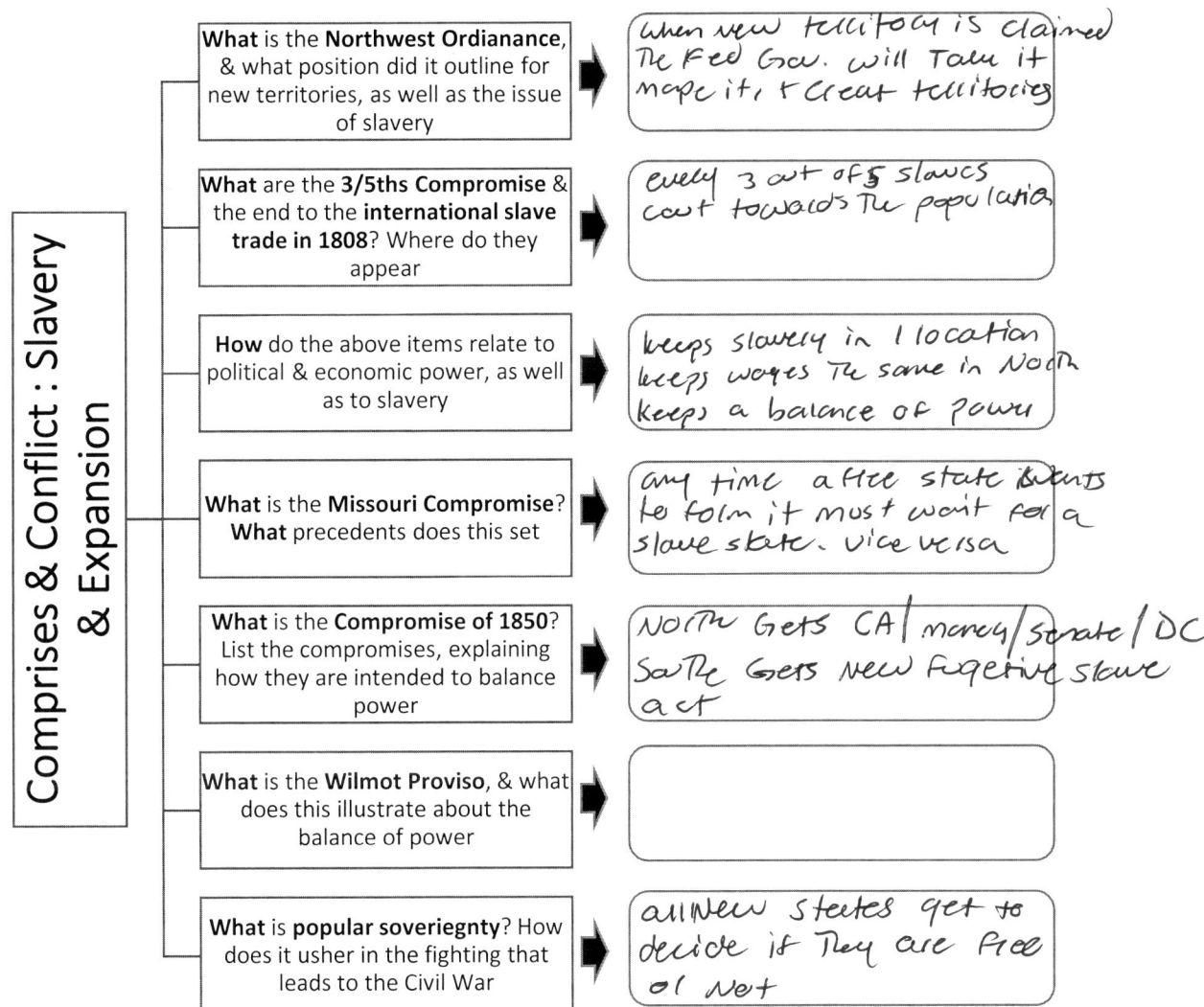

Comprises & Conflict : Slavery & Expansion

What is the **Northwest Ordianance**, & what position did it outline for new territories, as well as the issue of slavery	When new territory is claimed The Fed Gov. will Take it mape it, & Creat territories
What are the **3/5ths Compromise** & the end to the **international slave trade in 1808**? Where do they appear	every 3 out of 5 slaves cout towards The population
How do the above items relate to political & economic power, as well as to slavery	keeps slavery in 1 location keeps wages The same in North keeps a balance of power
What is the **Missouri Compromise**? **What** precedents does this set	any time a free state wants to form it must wait for a slave state. vice versa
What is the **Compromise of 1850**? List the compromises, explaining how they are intended to balance power	North Gets CA/ money/ senate/ DC South Gets New Fugetive slave act
What is the **Wilmot Proviso**, & what does this illustrate about the balance of power	
What is **popular soveriegnty**? How does it usher in the fighting that leads to the Civil War	all New states get to decide if They are free or Not

Each of these compromises addresses slavery (but not the suffering of slaves). What do they tell us is central to the conflict between the North & South? Why? How?

The Main concern is who has The power in The Senate + how can They keep up w/ Their Ideology

Name: _____

How does the escalation of violence between sub-groups of the North & South reveal ways in which both sides felt under siege by the other?

The traditional historical approach blamed the South for the Civil War, but over time some scholars "revived" the South through what is categorized as the Lost Cause, emphasizing Northern aggression.

Bleeding Kansas, 1856	Canning of Charles Sumner, 1856	John Brown's Attack on Harper's Ferry. 1859

How are these alike?

All involves ppl fighting for their Ideology

How do they differ?

ppl from North + South fight for keep Kanssas to be free or slave stut 2 Goves are Created	Charles Sumner Tally major Clay + gets his butt wemped	

Compare & contrast events involving violence leading up to the Civil War in the Venn Diagram. The intersecting circles should contain what they have in common.

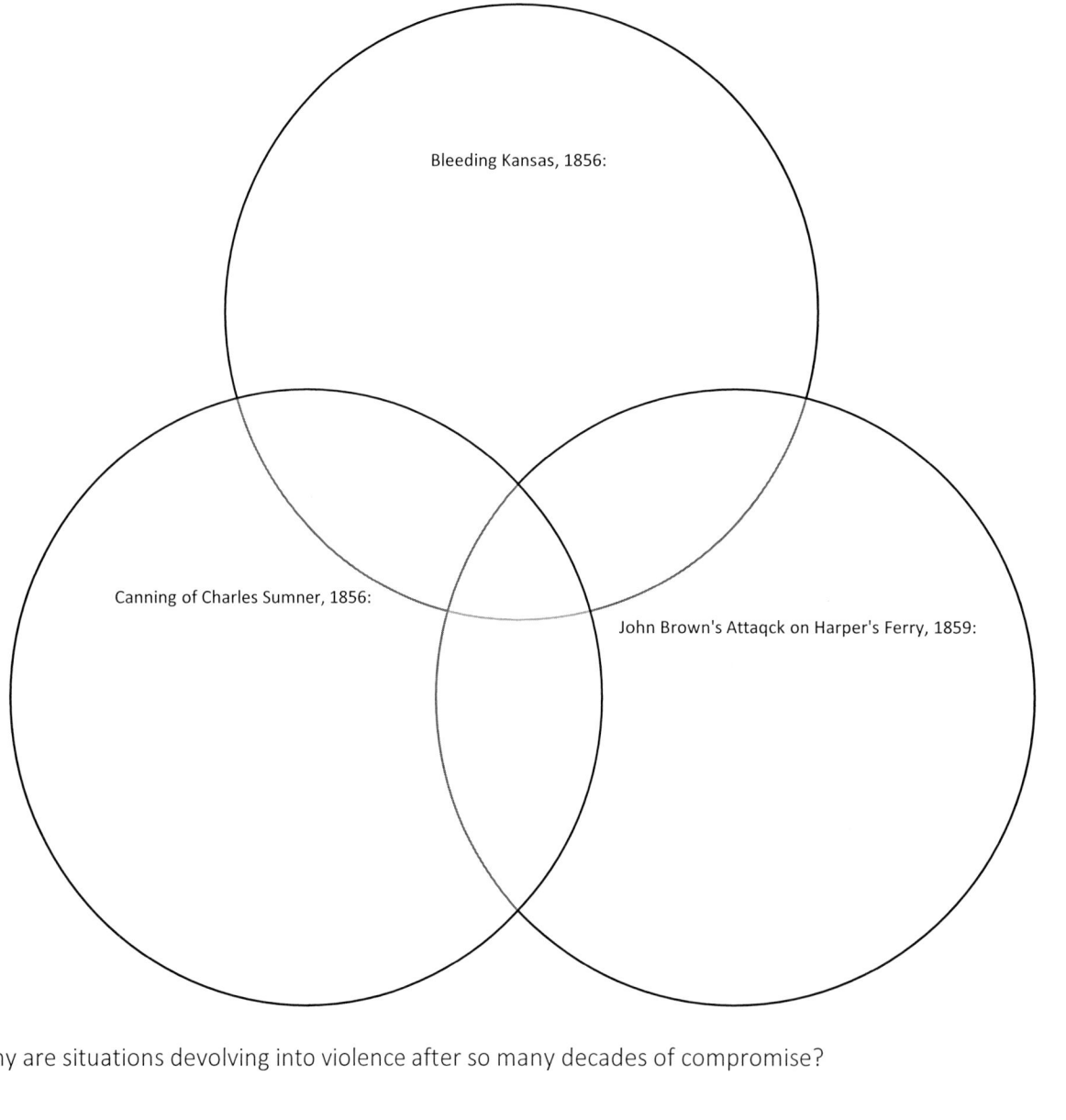

Bleeding Kansas, 1856:

Canning of Charles Sumner, 1856:

John Brown's Attaqck on Harper's Ferry, 1859:

Why are situations devolving into violence after so many decades of compromise?

_____

_____

_____

_____

Objective: to understand the significance of the Supreme Court's ruling in the Dred Scott case, pushing the nation towards war

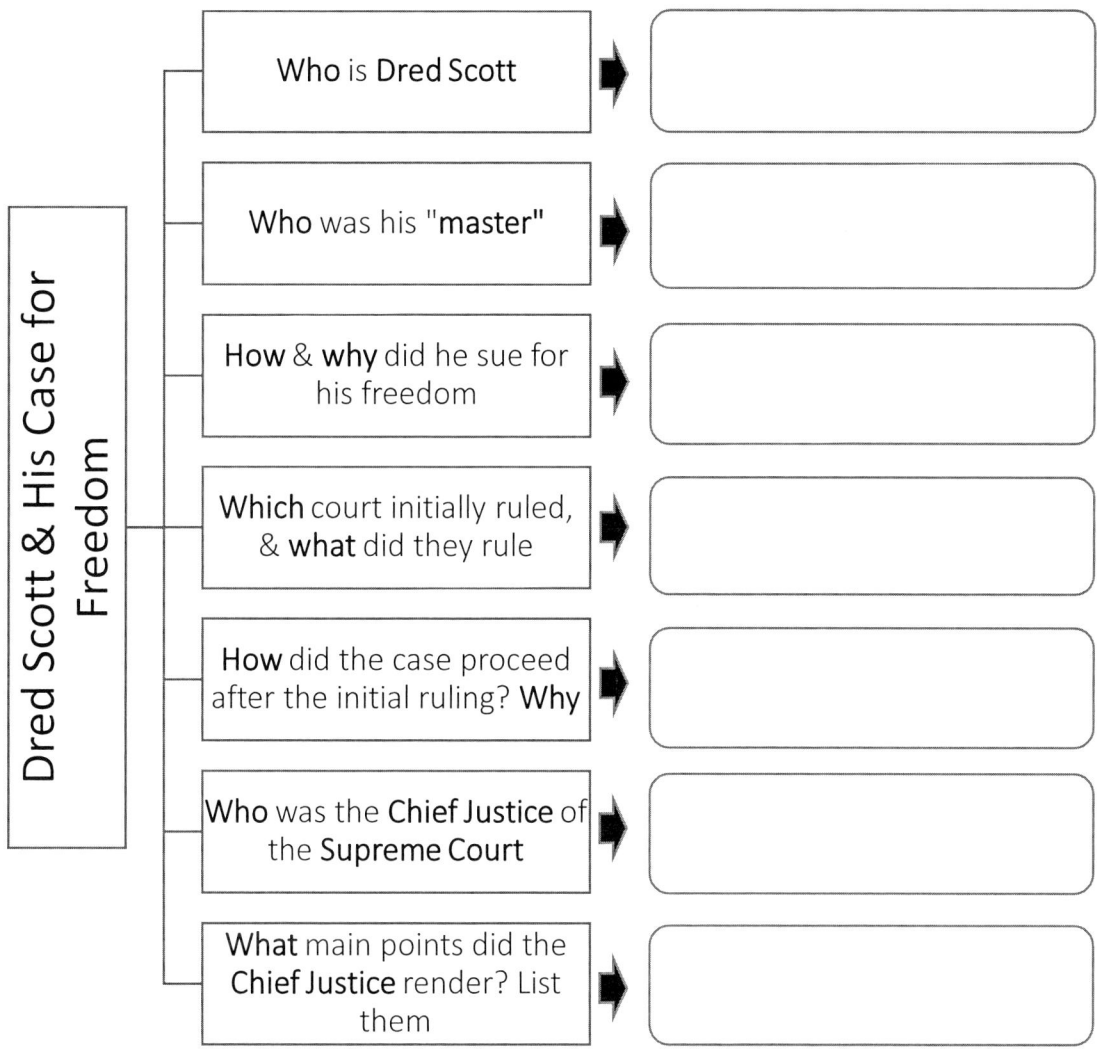

What is the significance of the ruling in Dred Scott case? How did the case impact all previous compromises holding the nation "together", and what became the Northern fear?

_____

_____

_____

Compare & contrast some events culminating in the Civil War using the Venn Diagram. The intersecting circles should contain what they have in common.

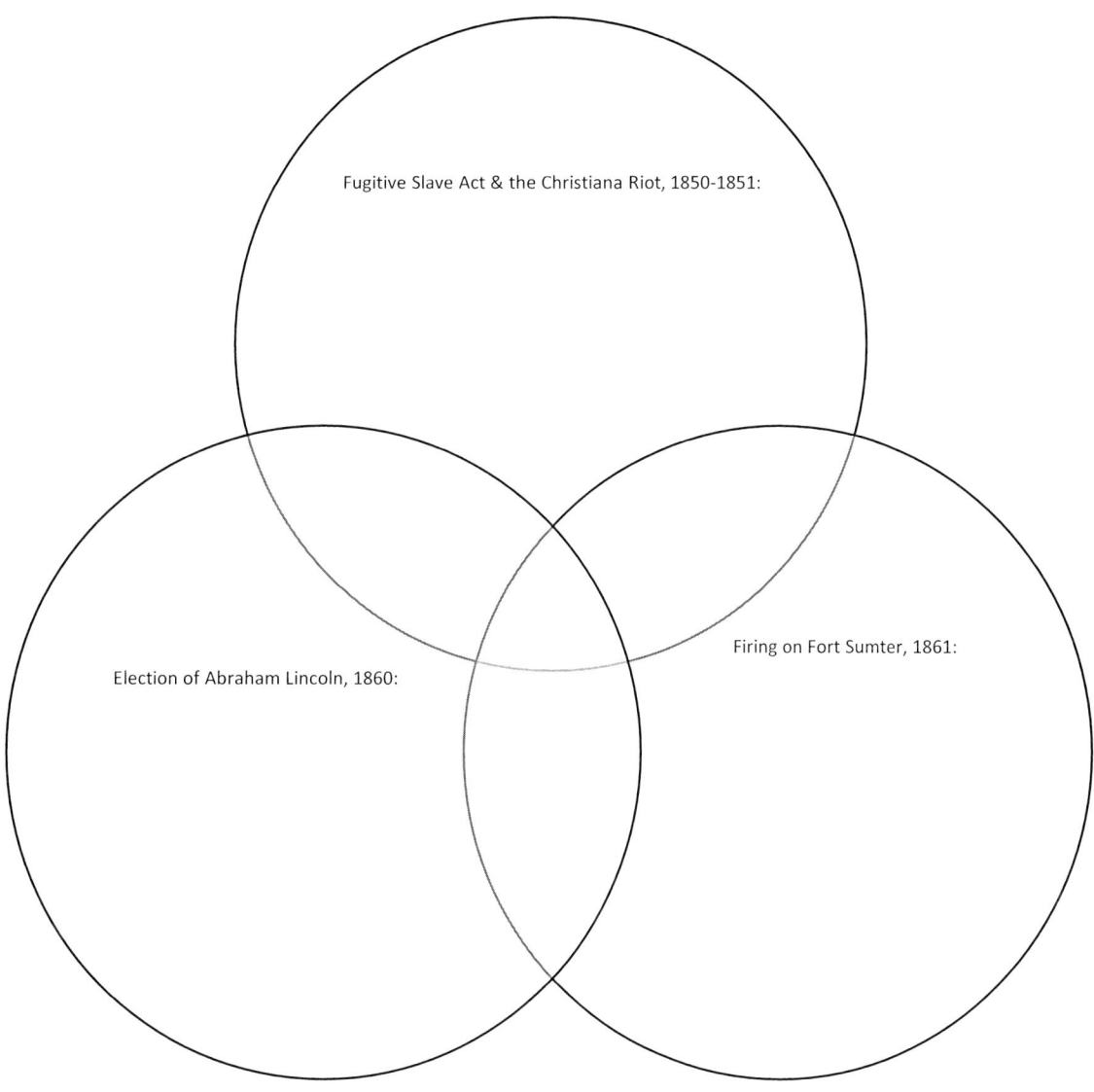

Fugitive Slave Act & the Christiana Riot, 1850-1851:

Election of Abraham Lincoln, 1860:

Firing on Fort Sumter, 1861:

How do each of these illustrate the inability of the South to exercise influence on a national level, leading to secession and, ultimately, war?

_____

_____

_____

_____

<u>Final Exam Study Guide</u>   Due Date: _____

This exam has two parts: Part I consists of the primary source analysis and outline forms. Part II contains your two essays. Everyone must write a short essay on the radicalism of the American Revolution. Then everyone will write a second essay answer to the question you choose to answer from the ones I select on exam day.

- Parts I is worth 50 points, 25 points for each primary source analysis form completed in advance of the final exam.
- Part II is 150 points, 50 points for your short essay, and 100 points for your long essay.
- Rules for Both Parts I and II
  - ➢ *The analysis forms, which you'll complete in advance at home are worth 50 points, 25 points each.* These analyses may be completed in groups as long you name all group members on each separately submitted form and each person contributes substantially.
  - ▪ <u>The essays, which you will write in class on the day of your exam are worth a combined total of 150 points.</u> **Be sure to bring one or two blank blue books from the BC bookstore.** Do not write on these at all until I tell you to.
  - ▪ You should use two to three primary sources that we examined throughout the semester that you can reference for analysis for each question.
  - ▪ I will select three possible questions on the day of the exam, and you will select one essay question and corresponding evidence/ primary sources. So you'll need to study at least three of the essay questions.
  - ▪ Reread your lecture notes and any relating texts.
  - ▪ Analyze the primary sources, filling out the analysis form as you go. You may do your own research and use different or additional primary sources.
    - ➢ You'll turn these in on the day of your test at the beginning of class.
    - ➢ You must also complete an outline. I have provided a template at the end of the primary source analysis form.
      - ✓ Remember, an outline should contain a thesis, sub claims, evidence/examples, and analysis/explanation. See me. I am always happy to help.
  - ▪ Arrive on time.
  - ▪ You may find many of my lecture notes and PowerPoint slides on my website, emillerbakersfieldcollege.weebly.com under Class Information, History 17A, Lecture Notes or PowerPoints. I am still posting the most recent ones.
    - ➢ My website password is Freed0m with a capital "F" and zero in place of an "o."
    - ➢ I want to remind you that I trust you to answer these questions in your own words. Don't simply copy words from the textbooks or from my notes. Imagine you're explaining the item or essay question to someone who asked you to teach them.

1 must be
5 para & formal intro & conclusion

Essay Questions: Two Primary Source Analysis Forms (50 points Combined) and Essays (150 points Combined)

<u>Required Essay Question</u>

On the day of the exam, everyone must write a short essay (3 paragraphs or more) to the question below. <u>You must answer with an argumentative essay.</u> Your answer must have a thesis, an introduction, several body paragraphs (at least 3), and a conclusion. **<u>You must underline your thesis</u>**. You must use each paragraph to argue in support of your thesis. These paragraphs should contain specific details and examples from reading, sources, and lecture. A helpful way to achieve this is by <u>using your key terms from lectures and readings for evidence.</u> These questions should be answered in historical terms, not according to events occurring today. If you wish to draw modern parallels, limit them to the contemporary significance in your conclusion.

1. Was the American Revolution radical? (Consider Gordon Wood, Charles Beard, historiography, the Articles of Confederation, the Constitution, Electoral College, Senate, Slavery, Class, Women's Rights, the Declaration of Independence, abolition, etc.)

<u>Additional Essay</u>

On the day of the exam, I will choose three of the questions below, and you will answer 1: <u>You must answer with an argumentative essay.</u> Your answer must have a thesis, an introduction, several body paragraphs (at least 3), and a conclusion. **<u>You must underline your thesis</u>**. You must use each paragraph to argue in support of your thesis. These paragraphs should contain specific details and examples from reading, sources, and lecture. A helpful way to achieve this is by <u>using your key terms from lectures and readings for evidence.</u> These questions should be answered in historical terms, not according to events occurring today. If you wish to draw modern parallels, limit them to the contemporary significance in your conclusion.

1. This is a two-part question. Was William Penn a hero or a hypocrite? Choose one or the other, hero or hypocrite, NOT BOTH. Did his faith enable the birth of American democracy?

2. Argue whose approach you believe would be better for both the greater number of Americans and the United States, Alexander Hamilton's or Thomas Jefferson's.

3. How could the North be both anti-slavery and racist? (more on the backside of this page)

4. What is the significance of the Dred Scott Case in understanding the unraveling of compromises that held the North and South together in the midst of westward expansion since 1787? (3/5th compromise, End of International Slave Trade in 1808, Missouri Compromise, Popular Sovereignty, etc.)

5. Who or what is to blame for the Civil War? Be careful if you choose this one. I am not providing primary sources of my choice. You will have to find your own and be very evidence-based.

BONUS ONLY:

1. Was America founded as a Christian nation?

<u>Remember you may use supplemental instruction or make an appointment with a history tutor through the tutoring center or writing to study for the test. You may also make one with a writing tutor at any of the available labs. I, of course, encourage you at attend SI. Submit proof of working with a tutor when you turn in your exam, and you get up to **5% extra credit** added to your test grade.</u>

General Tips:
- Brainstorm your ideas first. If you don't know how to do this, see me.
- Write your thesis.
- Come up with at least 3 sub-arguments that support your main thesis. These should function as your opening sentences in each of your body paragraphs. "A" essays will most likely have more than 3 sub-claims and more than 3 body paragraphs.
- List key terms from lecture notes or from the <u>A People and A Nation</u> chapter-reading study guides as evidence to support the sub-arguments/sub-claims that support your main thesis.
- Brain storm each of these key terms.
    3. "Bubbles" coming off of your key terms should outline all the details about the term as well as the significance.
    4. Create additional "brainstorm bubbles" off the details about the key terms. These "bubbles" should explain why/how you think these details, as well as the key term, support both your sub-argument and thesis.
- Now begin transforming all of these brainstormed details and explanations/analysis into paragraphs.
- Write your introduction last.
- Once you've written all the body paragraphs, write the conclusion. After that, rewrite your thesis. Most likely you'll better understand what your thesis/overall argument is once you've written all the body paragraphs and the conclusion.
- Once you recreate your thesis, write your introduction. State your thesis first. Underline it. Give a road map to your paper in your introduction as well. For example:

<u>The American Revolution increased the wealth and power of American elites who led the Revolution. This seems conservative, as if elite colonists overthrew Britain to bolster their own power. Nevertheless, the ideas created during this period eventually transformed American society and government; therefore, the American Revolution was, indeed, radical.</u> In order to support my claim about this radicalism, I first explain many historians' claims that economic and class interests reversed the radical ideals of the Revolution. Once I analyze this historical argument, I will examine the radical ideologies behind the Revolution. These include ideas about the equality of men, the right of the people to overthrow the government, and the ability of common men to understand and participate in politics. After showing how these ideas created new ways of viewing humanity and political rights, as well as the relationship between men and government, I will address four different historical events that show how these ideas radically transformed American society. These include an analysis of the *Declaration of Independence* and Thomas Paine's <u>Common Sense</u>, as well as Abigail Adams' assertions about the rights of women and the increased emergence of the abolition movement against slavery. By comparing the historical argument against the radicalism of the Revolution with historical evidence to the contrary, it is evident that the Revolution not only transformed American society and government, but it also changed the world. (This is not great writing, but hopefully it gives you an idea of what a thesis and introduction should include).

If you were to turn the above numbers 2 and 3, as well as the chart info into an outline, it would work something like this. (This part of the assignment is optional. You may complete the outline portion for extra credit, but I do not require you to do so.)

Below is only a model/suggestion. If it confuses you, don't use it.

(A Catchy Title that Engages and Reveals Your Thesis; Keep It Short)

I.   Introduction (A, B, and C for I can be in any order.)

    A.   Thesis statement from number 3 on the previous page

    B.   Context of the general topic

    C.   A road map to what you're going to cover/argue

II.   First Body Paragraph

    A.   1st sentence should be A, B, C, or D from number 1 on the previous page. (Remember, how you choose to arrange your evidence and arguments impacts the strength of your argument. Think about how Jennifer Morgan used Ligon as her first and last example to prove her point that initially he saw African women as human and female, and so on.) Box 4s from chart

    B.   Introduce your source from box 1 that corresponds with the box 4 you are using (A)

    C.   Quote and cite your evidence, or paraphrase it if you like. This comes from box 2 that corresponds with the box 4 you use (B). Use MLA, APA, or Chicago Manuel Style of Citation; it's up to you. Be consistent.
http://emillerbakersfieldcollege.weebly.com/help-with-citations.html

    D.   Summarize, Interpret, and Explain what the evidence meant to you/how you interpret it/how your understanding lead you to argue box 1B. This is called analysis.

III.   Second body Paragraph (Same process as II, but with different boxes)

IV.   Third Body Paragraph (Same process as II, but with different boxes)

V.   Fourth Body Paragraph (Same process as II, but with different boxes)

VI.   Conclusion

    A.   Convey the significance/implications of your argument.

    B.   Suggest further curiosities or possible future explorations.

Below is a template. OPTIONAL

(A Catchy Title that Engages and Reveals Your Thesis. Keep It Short)

I. Introduction (A, B, and C for I can be in any order.)

    A. Thesis

    _____

    _____

    _____

    _____

    _____

    B. General Context

    _____

    _____

    _____

    _____

    _____

    C. Road Map

    _____

    _____

    _____

    _____

    _____

II. First Body Paragraph

    A. 1st sentence Sub-claim

    _____

    _____

B. Introduce Your Source

_____

_____

_____

C. Quote & Cite/Paraphrase Your Evidence

_____

_____

_____

_____

_____

D. Summarize, Interpret, and Explain

_____

_____

_____

_____

_____

III. Second Body Paragraph (Same process as II, but with different boxes)

A. 1st sentence Sub-claim:

_____

_____

_____

_____

_____

B. Introduce Your Source

_____

_____

_____

_____

_____

_____

C. Quote & Cite/Paraphrase Your Evidence

_____

_____

_____

_____

_____

D. Summarize, Interpret, and Explain

_____

_____

_____

_____

_____

_____

_____

_____

IV. Third body Paragraph (Same process as II, but with different boxes)
    A. 1st sentence Sub-claim

_____

_____

_____

_____

_____

    B. Introduce Your Source

_____

_____

_____

_____

_____

    C. Quote & Cite/Paraphrase Your Evidence

_____

_____

_____

_____

_____

    D. Summarize, Interpret, and Explain

_____

_____

_____

_____

_____

_____

_____

_____

_____

_____

V. Fourth Body Paragraph (Same process as II, but with different boxes)

A. 1st sentence Sub-claim

_____

_____

_____

_____

_____

_____

B. Introduce Your Source

_____

_____

_____

_____

_____

C. Quote & Cite/Paraphrase Your Evidence

_____

_____

_____

_____

_____

_____

D. Summarize, Interpret, and Explain

_____

_____

_____

_____

_____

_____

VI. Conclusion

A. Convey the significance/implications of your argument:

_____

_____

_____

_____

_____

_____

B. Suggest further curiosities or possible future explorations:

_____

_____

_____

_____

_____

If you were to turn the above numbers 2 and 3, as well as the chart info into an outline, it would work something like this. (This part of the assignment is optional. You may complete the outline portion for extra credit, but I do not require you to do so.)

Below is a template. OPTIONAL

(A Catchy Title that Engages and Reveals Your Thesis. Keep It Short)

I. Introduction (A, B, and C for I can be in any order.)

    A. Thesis

        _____

        _____

        _____

        _____

    B. General Context

        _____

        _____

        _____

        _____

    C. Road Map

        _____

        _____

        _____

        _____

II. First Body Paragraph

    A. 1st sentence Sub-claim

        _____

        _____

_____

_____

_____

B. Introduce Your Source

_____

_____

_____

C. Quote & Cite/Paraphrase Your Evidence

_____

_____

_____

_____

_____

D. Summarize, Interpret, and Explain

_____

_____

_____

_____

_____

III. Second Body Paragraph (Same process as II, but with different boxes)

A. 1st sentence Sub-claim:

_____

_____

_____

B. Introduce Your Source

_____

C. Quote & Cite/Paraphrase Your Evidence

_____

D. Summarize, Interpret, and Explain

_____

IV. Third body Paragraph (Same process as II, but with different boxes)
    A. 1st sentence Sub-claim

_____

_____

_____

_____

_____

    B. Introduce Your Source

_____

_____

_____

_____

_____

    C. Quote & Cite/Paraphrase Your Evidence

_____

_____

_____

_____

_____

    D. Summarize, Interpret, and Explain

_____

_____

_____

_____

_____

_____

_____

_____

_____

_____

V. Fourth Body Paragraph (Same process as II, but with different boxes)

    A. 1st sentence Sub-claim

_____

_____

_____

_____

_____

    B. Introduce Your Source

_____

_____

_____

_____

    C. Quote & Cite/Paraphrase Your Evidence

_____

_____

_____

_____

_____

_____

D. Summarize, Interpret, and Explain

_____

_____

_____

_____

_____

_____

VI. Conclusion

A. Convey the significance/implications of your argument:

_____

_____

_____

_____

_____

B. Suggest further curiosities or possible future explorations:

_____

_____

_____

_____

_____

Student Notes

Student Notes

Student Notes

Student Notes

Student Notes

Student Notes

Student Notes

Student Notes

Student Notes

Student Notes

Student Notes